Welcome to the Won

D0475616

for:

May God's love surround you today,
tomorrow and always.

from:

Ephesians 1:2
I pray that God our Father and our Lord Jesus Christ will be kind to
you and will bless you with peace!
(Contemporary English Version)

Have you reached the wonder years yet?

I wonder why you care, GOD – why do you bother with us at all?
Psalm 144: 3 (The Message)

●

Just call me Wonder Woman! Not because I am a superhero ready to save the world – but simply because I spend ten minutes every day standing and wondering… I wonder where I left my keys? I wonder if I charged my phone? I wonder if I have enough petrol? I wonder where my glasses are? I wonder where I parked the car? I wonder why I opened the fridge?

YES, I think I've finally reached THE WONDER YEARS. How about you?

This status didn't suddenly happen overnight, but crept up on me slowly one muddle-aged mix-up at a time. First came the morning I had to text my daughter because I couldn't stop wondering whether I had turned off the iron. Then, there was the occasion I turned the car around and drove home simply to check if I'd remembered to lock the front door. And then there was the time that I wondered where my phone was and found it in the freezer. *Don't ask!* For me, it's often a short hop from wondering to full-blown worrying and I hate to spend my day worrying. I'd rather double-check that everything is safe and secure and move on to the next big thing.

A while ago I heard about two medical students who left their student house and forgot to turn the iron off – not just for an evening, nor even for a weekend, but for the entire Christmas holiday! It's a wonder their flat was still standing in January. And this story is exactly why I feel the need to keep double-checking – if brainy young medics can forget to turn off the iron then what chance does a middle-aged matron suffering from BLS (Busy Life Syndrome) have?

God must throw up his hands in despair when he sees how scatty and forgetful we are – or as the psalmist says "I wonder why he bothers with us at all." But God's love is unchanging, his care is unceasing and his understanding is unending. He loves us totally – complete with all our muddle and mistakes. And no matter how many times we wonder *What did I come upstairs for?* or *Did I turn the gas off?* – we need never ever wonder whether God still loves us because we are promised that his love is eternal. Isn't that AWESOME?

And now, I wonder if it's time to stop typing and check if I switched off the iron…

Father God, thank you for your patience with us,
even when we're muddled and disorganised.
No matter what else we forget, help us to remember
that you love us and understand us.

Twice blessed

God can bless you with everything you need, and you will always have more than enough to do all kinds of good things for others.
2 Corinthians 9:8 (CEV)

•

Have you ever forgotten a close friend's birthday? It's embarassing isn't it? You don't want them to think you don't care, but there's no escaping the fact that you've missed their special day.

Not so long ago, the opposite happened to me. I didn't forget a friend's birthday, I simply forgot that I had already remembered it – until I received a slightly perplexed thank-you note.

Thank you for the birthday gifts.
Did you realise that you sent me two lots of presents?

And then I remembered that in a particularly organised moment, and in order to save the postage as she lives some miles away, I had taken her present to a barbecue in July and left it with her to open in September. Wow! Thinking ahead. So organised and so out of character.

Then, September arrived and off I went to choose, buy, wrap and dispatch another present for the postie to deliver on her actual birthday. Forgetful, or what? But then again, perhaps it's rather nice to be remembered twice. Two presents equals twice the enjoyment, but don't tell everyone or all my friends will expect similar treatment!

Double the gifts. Double the love. Double the blessings. God blesses us in just the same way, and more so, not just with a double portion, but with abundant blessings. He enfolds us, surrounds us, wraps us in his love and care every single day – not just once a year. His amazing love is a wonderful gift to be enjoyed every day.

*Lord, your blessings come wrapped in love and
not just on our birthday, but every day. Thank you.*

You are never too old...

To pop the bubble wrap

To fly a kite

To play Pooh sticks

To have an advent calendar

To scrape out the cake bowl

To build a snowman

To eat candyfloss

To blow bubbles

You are never too old...

To paddle in the sea

To ride on a carousel

To wonder at a rainbow

To smell the roses

To daydream

To enjoy a Christmas stocking

To make popcorn

To flip a pancake

And don't let anyone tell you otherwise!

●

You are never too old to set another goal or to dream a new dream.

Les Brown *(1945–present day), American businessman*

A channel for God's love

But I am giving you a new command.
You must love each other, just as I have loved you.
If you love each other, everyone will know that you are my disciples.
John 13:34-35 (CEV)

'The man of the house is the master of the remote control' is one of the unwritten laws of modern life, along with 'Woe to the woman who comes between a man and his remote'. My dearly beloved can be snoring his head off in front of his favourite TV programme, but the moment I surreptitiously pick up the remote and change channels his head jolts up and his eyes open quicker than you can say 'BBC One'.

On the other hand... 'A man who mislays the remote is like a chicken without a head.' My husband is powerless when the aforementioned gadget goes astray or, worse still, malfunctions. Needless to say, it's always my fault. It is suggested that I must have done something to it because, "It was working fine yesterday."

There follows much pressing of buttons, in case it might suddenly work at the 303rd attempt. Amidst the bewilderment, we approach the TV with a torch and peer at the casing of the magic telly box, trying, in our increasing short-sightedness, to locate the exceptionally well-camouflaged control panel. Then, of course, we press the wrong button and the picture and/or sound disappears and it's a case of which-one-did-we-just-press because we need to press it again to get the sound and picture back!

By the time we actually find the channel we want (complete with sound and vision), we're either in such a strop that we're not speaking to one another or the programme is over and we're left wondering if it might have been quicker – not to mention healthier for our relationship – to have bought a new TV.

There are a few people who think that becoming a Christian means turning into some kind of robot, directed by an unseen deity with a high-powered remote control! The reality couldn't be further from the truth. God created us – he knows how we work and he loves us personally and deeply. Happily, we all have the potential to channel his loving kindness for the good of everyone. To follow Jesus means to allow him to tune us, removing our imperfections, so that we can present the high definition reality of his love for us. Get the picture! AC

Creator of all, help me to show the people in my life just how much you care about them. Help me to transmit a clear picture of your love.

Out with the old, in with the new

Christ died to rescue those who had sinned and broken the old agreement.
Now he brings his chosen ones a new agreement with its guarantee of
God's eternal blessings!
Hebrews 9:15 (CEV)

●

Me get an iPhone? No way! My trusty 'text and talk-only' mobile was good enough for me, thank you very much. My daughters and their partners might be gadget geeks but I was digging in my heels, despite their attempts to convert me.

Yes, of course it must be handy to take photos on your phone but what was wrong with a camera? As for the internet, I had the laptop for sending emails and surfing. Why on Earth would I ever need to look up something in the middle of a supermarket or deep in a forest?

If you have grown-up children, you know how convincing they can be. If they also have tech-savvy partners who can blind you with the benefits, you stand absolutely no chance. So it was that I became the proud owner of an iPhone.

I'm converted! My new iPhone is more than just a phone, it's a whole new way of life. It's so useful if you need a map in a strange town, or you want to compare the price of something when you're out and about. I can see my daughters live on screen when I use 'FaceTime' and the camera is just as good as my trusty digital. In fact, when my daughter gave birth to my granddaughter, my son-in-law announced her safe arrival by texting me a photo of their brand new baby. I was able to see her before I heard about her. How wonderful was that?

A lot of us are resistant to change, especially if we are content with the old way of doing things. When Jesus came to live among men, the rulers and authorities of the day were far from happy. Until then, the ordinary people who believed in God danced to the rulers' tune and obeyed the religious laws they had created and then enforced. Jesus told people that God is more interested in the attitude of their hearts than he is in rules and rituals. His teaching was like a breath of fresh air and it led to a brand new way of living that set people free from stifling regulations. Some people needed convincing, but once they had invited Jesus into their lives they were joyfully converted and there was no turning back. Bit like me and my iPhone really!

AC

Thank you Father, for sending your son to show us a new way of living and being. Your way opens the door and sets us free!

*I have decided to follow Jesus, no turning back, no turning back.
The cross before me, the world behind me, no turning back, no turning back.*
Sadhu Sundar Singh *(1889–1929), Indian Christian missionary*

I'm not old!

I'm not old, I'm vintage.

•

I'm not old, I'm a valuable antique.

•

I'm not old, I'm a rare classic.

•

I'm not old, I just need some WD40.

•

I'm not old, I'm retro.

•

I'm not old, I'm just a little frayed at the edges.

•

I'm not old, I'm just well-travelled.

•

I'm not old, I haven't even had my mid-life crisis yet!

•

I'm not old, I demand a recount!

•

I'm not old, well not geologically speaking!

I'm not old,
I'm a recycled teenager.

17th-century Nun's Prayer

•

*Lord, Thou knowest better than I know myself that I am growing older
and will someday be old.*

*Keep me from the fatal habit of thinking I must say something
on every subject and on every occasion.*

Release me from craving to straighten out everybody's affairs.

Make me thoughtful but not moody; helpful but not bossy.

*With my vast store of wisdom, it seems a pity not to use it all,
but Thou knowest, Lord, that I want a few friends at the end.*

*Keep my mind free from the recital of endless details; give me wings to get
to the point. Seal my lips on my aches and pains. They are increasing,
and love of rehearsing them is becoming sweeter as the years go by.*

*I dare not ask for grace enough to enjoy the tales of others' pains,
but help me to endure them with patience.*

*I dare not ask for improved memory, but for a growing humility and a lessening
cocksureness when my memory seems to clash with the memories of others.
Teach me the glorious lesson that occasionally I may be mistaken.*

*Keep me reasonably sweet; I do not want to be a Saint –
some of them are so hard to live with – but a sour old person
is one of the crowning works of the devil.*

*Give me the ability to see good things in unexpected places, and talents in
unexpected people. And, give me, O Lord, the grace to tell them so.*

Amen

Author unknown

A lesson in selfies from a Stormtrooper

May the grace of the Lord Jesus Christ, and the love of God,
and the fellowship of the Holy Spirit be with you all.
2 Corinthians 13:14 (NIV)

●

One Saturday, I woke up in a hotel in Cardiff and went down for breakfast only to discover that Stormtroopers had taken over the foyer. It's a funny old world and I had walked right into the middle of a geeky sci-fi convention. I have only seen one *Star Wars* movie right through, and my son had to explain the back story to me, so the thrill of this experience was a little wasted on me. Though I did find it incredibly funny when they all trooped into the bar to buy drinks, only to discover that they couldn't even wet their lips with their masks on.

I snapped a few photos on my new phone from the top of the stairs. Then, minutes later, Darth Vader walked out of the bedroom opposite. It was quite surreal, he must have been seven foot tall and his loud ominous breathing and menacing voice were simply awesome. Apparently, they created his voice by placing a microphone in front of a scuba-tank regulator. Well, there's something I didn't know before.

Later, as I elbowed my way to the exit, I grinned at several Stormtroopers on the way out and one put his arm around me. "Go on," he said. "Take a selfie, you know you want to!" Ah...a selfie, yes that would be novel, but err … I had to explain that I'm muddle-aged, with a new phone, and up until this bizarre moment I hadn't really felt the need to take a selfie. And, this is embarrassing, I'm not even sure how to do it!

No worries, this elite warrior of the Galactic Empire gave me a quick lesson on my new phone and in seconds a copy of my selfie was winging its way to my son at Uni on the other side of the country. Who's a clever mum now, eh? I bet no one else in the history of the Galactic Empire has been taught how to take a selfie by a Stormtrooper.

"May the Force be with you," said my stormtrooping friends in farewell. "And may God be with you," I thought. And in my head I heard the words of The Grace that is so often shared in church: *May the grace of the Lord Jesus Christ, and the love of God, and the fellowship of the Holy Spirit be with you all.* And I could sense God smiling.

Jesus, thank you for all the fun and unexpected things that happen every day. Thank you that wherever we are, and whoever we meet, you are always alongside us.

Abundant Blessings

Blessed are those who are young at heart, but slightly older in other places.

•

Blessed are those who plan to make
the rest of their life the best of their life.

•

Blessed are those who learn something new every day, even if they forget
half a dozen other things forever.

•

Blessed are those who rise and shine every morning, even if they can no longer
do both at the same time.

•

Blessed are those who have discovered that embarrassing the kids
is just one more parenting skill they can offer.

•

Blessed are those who count their blessings not their birthdays.

•

Blessed are those who snuggle and hug, spoil and indulge, boast and brag,
for they shall be called GRANDPARENTS.

•

Blessed are those who talk to themselves – they evidently need an expert opinion.

•

Blessed are those who are old enough to make their own decisions…
but not young enough to remember what they decided.

•

Blessed are those who can laugh at themselves because, as they get older,
they will never cease to be amused.

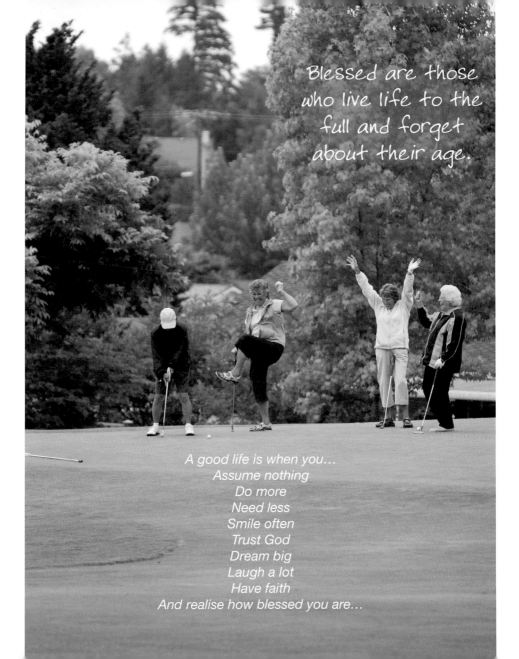

Blessed are those who live life to the full and forget about their age.

A good life is when you...
Assume nothing
Do more
Need less
Smile often
Trust God
Dream big
Laugh a lot
Have faith
And realise how blessed you are...

Savour the flavour

There is a time for everything, and a season for every activity under the heavens.
Ecclesiastes 3:1 (NIV)

•

Mature people like me – oh, let's be honest, older people like me – can remember the thrill when the first fresh strawberries of the year appeared, in June or July, depending on the weather. The taste was wonderful, particularly if you'd gone into the fields and picked your own. Hunting the ripest, reddest, juiciest fruit, and then that slightly guilty feeling of clandestinely popping one into your mouth as you picked. Bliss on the taste buds; sweet and slightly acid together.

Yesterday, they were selling strawberries in the greengrocer's. In January. Strawberries in winter. A bit pricey, but tempting in their plastic boxes. Where do they come from? Certainly not local fields. They'll have been flown in or trucked over from Israel or Spain. Or wherever.

But is it such a good idea? When you can get something all the time, whatever the season, the thrill goes. They're not special anymore. There's no excitement – they're just strawberries. In wanting everything, all the time, we lose the rhythm of life. God gives us winter and summer, spring and autumn. Darkness and light. Times of shortage, times of plenty. Waiting for harvest. It's those blank times, when we're just waiting, that makes the fulfilment so full of flavour.

Lord of the seasons, I want to be content with what I have,
to take life as it comes and yearn for nothing else but you.

Eddie Askew *(1927–2007)*
Christian writer and former International Director of The Leprosy Mission,
from Chasing the Leaves

Made up for life

... the LORD said to him, "Pay no attention to how tall and handsome he is.
I have rejected him, because I do not judge as people judge.
They look at the outward appearance, but I look at the heart."
1 Samuel 16:7 (GNT)

●

One muddle-aged friend carefully applies her make up every morning before she greets the world. On one especially busy day, she applied eye liner, eye shadow and mascara to her right eye and then flew out of the house and off to work at top speed. Her colleagues were amused and intrigued by her lopsided appearance! She is now obsessed by checking the mirror before meeting the world.

None of us likes seeing our ageing reflection every morning, but there's very little we can do about it. I can remember when my skin was smooth and taut, when I could pinch the skin on the back of my hand and it would silently 'ping' back into place before I had time to blink. Today it's more of a relaxed fit. And as for my face, these days I have to make sure I get up in time for it to settle. At this rate I'll be getting up before I go to bed if I'm to be fit to be seen the next day! Wouldn't it be great if we could just pop in the tumble drier and come out wrinkle-free and a size smaller?

Our appearance, whether we are happy with it or not, can't disguise what's on the inside. It's what is in our heart that counts, the way that we treat other people and our attitude to life.

In a letter to the Romans, the apostle Paul wrote, '…fix your attention on God. You'll be changed from the inside out. Readily recognise what he wants from you, and quickly respond to it... God brings the best out of you…' *Romans 12:2* (The Message)

We don't have to copy what the rest of the world does. We don't have to struggle to be the person the world expects us to be. It will only make us unhappy. God, on the other hand, is a father who encourages us to be the person we were born to be, and that puts a smile on our face that's far too beautiful to cover up.

Thank you Lord, that when your beauty shines from within us, we don't need to pretend to be anything other than what we are.

Wrinkles should merely indicate
where smiles have been.

Mark Twain 1835–1910, American writer

If my memory was any worse,
I could plan my own surprise party.

Memory Matters

My wife has a terrible memory; she never forgets a single thing.

My memory, on the other hand, is excellent – apart from three things:
faces, names and… something else.

•

Of course, the advantage to your memory being less sharp is that you can watch
repeats on BBC and you don't remember watching them before.

•

I still have a photographic memory, but it no longer offers same day service.

•

Perhaps I have Teflon disease – nothing seems to stick in my mind.

•

My memory's not as reliable as it used to be.
Also, my memory's not as reliable as it used to be.

•

When you meet people, if you can't remember their names just call them stranger.
"Hello stranger, long time no see!"

•

I had amnesia once – or maybe twice.

•

Even my bed has a better memory than me –
thanks to its memory foam mattress.

Have a God day!

May the LORD who created the heavens and the earth give you his blessing.
Psalm 115:15 (CEV)

●

Sometimes I think my phone is smarter than me! It can calculate sums, look up maps, give me a weather report and tell me what time a film is showing at the cinema. And when it comes to texting it can often predict exactly which word I want to use. Clever eh?

The only trouble is that sometimes it predicts entirely the wrong word. Rather like the lady who sent her husband a birthday text…

> *Happy birthday to you*
> *Happy birthday to you*
> *Happy Birthday dead husband*
> *Happy birthday to you.*

"Thanks," he replied. "I really hope you meant dear!"

Ahhhh.

Then there's the mum who texted her daughter 'Exams OK?' only to receive the surprising answer 'Yep - no pancake attacks', followed a moment later by 'Oops sorry, PANIC attacks. No panic attacks.'

I decided to finish a text the other day with the words *Have a good day.* But for some obscure reason my phone sent *Have a God day.* When I stop to think about it, I rather like that greeting.

'May you have a God day, filled with his love and blessings.
May you enjoy the beauty of his creation and feel his presence in your life today.'

Yes that works for me. Some mistakes are worth embracing. Have a God day!

*Lord, thank you for 'God days' when we feel your presence,
enjoy your creation and know your love intimately.
May we have many, many days just like that.*

With perseverance and determination...

… And we must be determined to run the race that is ahead of us.
We must keep our eyes on Jesus, who leads us and makes our faith complete…
Hebrews 12:1-2 (CEV)

•

My mother has just reached a milestone birthday. She may not thank me for divulging her age, but it's only one more decade before she receives a royal telegram. She's a feisty lady and over the years, she has taught me many lessons on how to grow old successfully, some silly, some sensible. Here are just a few…

Lesson 1: *Always remember that age doesn't matter unless you're a cheese.*
(Mum – you're a splendid old cheddar!)

Lesson 2: *When you bend down to tie up your shoe laces, stop and think if there's anything else you can do while you're down there.*

Lesson 3: *Pause to celebrate if you remember what you came upstairs for, without first having to return back downstairs to think again.*

Lesson 4: *Always be willing to try new things – it needn't be bungee jumping, it could just be a new flavour of biscuit!*

Lesson 5: *Whatever you do, do it with style and aplomb – and if you haven't got a plomb, try a peach or a banana!*

Lesson 6: *Never forget that old age is a wonderful time for outrage. Make it your aim to do something outrageous every week.*

Lesson 7: *Make a point of learning new things – anyone who stops learning is old whether they are 19 or 90.*

Lesson 8: *No matter how old you are, never give up, keep pushing through. Don't stop doing things just because they're a little bit harder than last year.*

●

My mother is a terrific *(and occasionally terrifying)* example of pushing on and pushing through. Like many of her generation who lived through the war, she demonstrates an inner Blitz Spirit. Don't give up, don't give in, keep on trying, and 'make do and mend'. Stoicism and Determination are her middle names, even when sometimes they are spelt STUBBORN.

Seriously though, it's commendable to be determined and, if we keep our eyes on Jesus, he will be our motivation to keep going and our companion for the journey. He will encourage us, support us and give us the strength to complete the race. Happy are those who live life to the full.

JM

Father God, we don't want to live half-heartedly.
Show us how to live life to the full, finding the fun in every day,
and embracing every new opportunity with perseverance and determination.

You are old school if...

You sat at a wooden desk with a lift-up lid and a china inkwell and you used blotting paper to mop up inky mistakes.

●

You were taught the 3 Rs: Reading, Writing and Arithmetic. In fact it's one R, one W and an A, but that's what our schools taught us so it must be right.

●

You remember chalk and talk, not smart boards and iPads.

●

You remember being a milk monitor, collecting a crate of miniature glass bottles, and then putting a straw in each one.

●

You learnt to tie a proper tie, no new-fangled, clip-on ties for you.

●

You remember school dinners with delicacies like 'fly cemetery pudding' and jam roly poly.

●

You gave in handwritten homework in a tatty exercise book – no typing and emailing homework in your day.

●

You remember when the teacher would throw the board rubber or chalk at anyone not concentrating.

●

You played hopscotch, cat's cradle, conkers, marbles, jacks and British bulldog in the playground – no one played games on a mobile phone.

The best days of your life

You graduated from school without any help from GOOGLE or Wikipedia.
And that deserves RESPECT.

Dependence day

Then Jesus called the children over to him and said to the disciples,
"Let the little children come to me! Never send them away! For the Kingdom of God
belongs to men who have hearts as trusting as these little children's. And anyone
who doesn't have their kind of faith will never get within the Kingdom's gates."
Luke 18:16-17 (TLB)

When I was a teenager, I was amused when my mother insisted on turning on the light to read or thread a needle. I laughed when older people complained about sitting in a draught. Draught? What draught? An open door doesn't mean there's a draught; it's just *air*. And as for a golden oldie asking me to unscrew the lid of a jar – well, it was a chance for me to show off my superior strength.

None of the above frailties would ever come to me. *My* body become weaker and less efficient? *No way!* I'd have 20/20 vision forever; I'd never complain about a draught (unless my opponent was cheating in a game of them) and my strength would never diminish. All this nonsense about being less able to do this, that and the other was utter codswallop; the negative mind-set of an older generation. Oh the misplaced confidence of youth.

Move forward a few decades and... err... I can put my hand up to all the above. Am I embarrassed? Well, not really. I wear my glasses like a badge of wisdom. I've discovered that draughts really *do* exist and I'm happy to let a young whippersnapper show off their superior strength when I need a jar opening.

Acknowledging one's inability to deal with everything, whatever the reason, can be hard. It requires us to swallow our pride and allow others to help. An elderly lady I know says it's no wonder old age is classed as second childhood; the older she gets the more help she needs with dressing and walking!

Jesus said we must become like little children to enter the Kingdom of Heaven. In other words, we need to swallow our pride and accept his guiding hand, depend on his love and support, and trust that he knows best. And while we're at it, perhaps we should gratefully accept help from friends and family, and even say thank you with a gracious smile!

AC

*Lord, I am such a stubborn creature, help me to know
when it's right to accept help and then to do so graciously.*

Sat nav savvy

The way to become wise is to honour the LORD;
he gives sound judgment to all who obey his commands.
He is to be praised forever.
Psalm 111:10 (GNT)

●

A sign in my local supermarket car park said 'THIEVES WANT YOUR SAT NAV!'
'Well, they can get lost,' I thought.

I sometimes wonder what I did before sat nav. How on Earth did I get from A to B without asking a machine to give me directions? Like a genie in a magic lamp, I tell the unseen owner of the voice my desired destination and *hey presto,* it takes me there! It even tells me how long it should take and how many miles the journey will be.

It is so easy to depend upon something that has been designed to make life simpler for us. Anything that takes away the need to spend time researching and planning sounds almost too good to be true. Sometimes it is.

Actually, I'm not quite as trusting as I sound. While I use sat nav for long unfamiliar journeys, I also love looking at maps and planning trips the old fashioned way. It pays to have a Plan B; I've seen too many items on the local news where lorries have become wedged between houses because their drivers believed everything their sat nav told them.

Did you hear about the bird watchers at Gibraltar Point in Lincolnshire? They looked on in total amazement when a Syrian truck driver arrived in his 32-tonne vehicle. He was actually looking for the Island of Gibraltar and had made a 1,600-mile detour from his intended destination! Sometimes, you really need a good old fashioned road atlas to reveal the whole picture.

It's a bit like life in general, really. It's so tempting to look for quick-fix solutions to problems. It's easy to take short cuts which appear to save us time but which wind up creating additional obstacles. We can be too quick to take advice from unreliable sources in our rush to get where we want to be.

God gave us the Bible as the ultimate guide book. Like an atlas, it shows us the bigger picture and reading it regularly helps us to hear God's directions for our life. It's easy to leave it on the shelf gathering dust, but God will direct us through the wisdom it contains, if we ask him to do so.

In you alone I put my trust, Lord.
You are my guide, help me to hear your directions.

Two Swedish holidaymakers were attempting to reach the island of Capri but ended up 400 miles away in an industrial town at the other end of Italy after mistakenly typing 'Carpi' into their sat nav!
A man from the Carpi regional government said: "It's hard to understand how they managed it. I mean, Capri is an island! The travellers were surprised, rather than angry. They just got back in their car and started driving south."

Sat Nav Stories

A word of advice.... Do not set your 'Home' address on your sat nav to your actual address. This is in case someone steals your car. They'll know you're out and can then proceed to ransack your property. Instead, set the 'Home' address to that of your local police station. That'll teach 'em!

●

My wife bought me a Bon Jovi sat nav. Thankfully, we're halfway there!

●

A Belgian truck driver blamed his sat nav after leaving a £20,000 trail of destruction in his wake in Wadebridge, Cornwall. Directed by his sat nav into a tight cul-de-sac, the unfortunate trucker panicked and put his foot down. He ended his turning manoeuvre by ploughing over a mini roundabout, getting a car trapped under his lorry and destroying five more vehicles.

●

I think my sat nav is shortsighted. We went to our local Safari Park and it said 'Bear left!' when it was quite clearly a giraffe.

●

A Yorkshire policeman had his sat nav stolen. A spokesman said he was searching for Leeds.

●

Someone stole my sat nav. Now my whole life lacks direction.

●

A chauffeur drove his luxury vehicle down a flight of steps in a busy Austrian city centre after his sat nav told him it was OK to do so. Thinking he'd be able to park right outside the front door of a shop, he descended the steps with his boss in the back seat. He lost his job but now works as an air-traffic controller. How scary is that!

Random acts of kindness

There was a believer in Joppa named Tabitha (which in Greek is Dorcas).
She was always doing kind things for others and helping the poor.

Acts 9:36 (NLT)

•

My friend Loraine is an incredibly busy lady and she packs a lot into her hectic life.
One day she arrived at the supermarket thinking, 'I really must do something about
my back window. I can hardly see out and the windscreen wipers are barely making
any difference.'

As she scooted up and down the supermarket aisles, she spotted a spray bottle of
window cleaner and popped that in her basket along with some kitchen towel thinking,
'There's no time like the present, I'll clean the window before I set off home.'

Arriving at her car, she put her shopping on the ground, took out the spray and
thoroughly cleaned the back window. Job done. She could now see clearly through
the glass and right into the car. 'Strange, I don't have a coat like that,' she thought as
she peered into the car, 'and my seats are a different colour.'

Oops! In her haste to get the job done, she had cleaned the wrong car, which was
parked just a couple of spaces away from hers. It's an easy mistake to make.

She moved on and started again, and this time she cleaned the side windows as well,
because if a job's worth doing it's worth doing properly. As she looked through the
sparkling clean side windows, she spotted something on the back seat that didn't
belong to her. Uh oh! Once again she had cleaned the wrong car. It was the right
colour, but a different make. There, just a few spaces away, was her own car quietly
waiting for its windows to be cleaned.

"So," we asked, "did you finally clean your own car?" "No way," said Loraine. "I didn't
want people to think that I was some manic woman going round cleaning random cars
that didn't belong to me. I drove home and cleaned my car when it was safely parked
on my own driveway!"

What about the two folk who had their cars cleaned? I wonder what they thought about this random act of kindness. Hopefully, they noticed the improvement and felt pleased, while perhaps a little mystified by how it had happened. And I'm sure that God was amused as he watched Loraine clean not just one but two wrong cars!

Now I wonder what secret, random act of kindness I could do for someone today? Maybe I'll clean the car while I think about it....

Lord, a small act of kindness makes the world a happier place.
Help me to find a way to bring a smile to someone's face today.

Car crisis

Don't jump to conclusions – there may be a perfectly good explanation
for what you just saw.
Proverbs 25:8 (The Message)

•

Brian was just leaving a work conference that had been held at a town centre hotel
when he discovered that he didn't have his car keys. He checked his pockets,
but no joy. Then he returned to the conference room and searched all around, but
again nothing…

Suddenly he realised that he might well have left his keys in the car. He rushed off to the car park, hoping against hope that he hadn't left them in the ignition, or sticking out of the boot as he had done once or twice before. His kids would really tease him if they found out. And his wife was always telling him to be more careful as one day someone would certainly steal the car. Sadly, the car park was almost empty and there was no sign of his red Ford Mondeo. It must have been stolen.

Downhearted, Brian went back into the hotel and called the police, feeling more than a little embarrassed. He gave them his location, admitting that he had most likely left his keys in the car and, as a result, it had been stolen. Then, he ordered a restoring cup of tea in the hotel lounge and sat down to think what he should do next. Twenty minutes later, he remembered that he'd better ring his wife, Brenda, and explain he'd be late. "Darling," he confessed, "I've been incredibly stupid and left my keys in the car and now it's been stolen."

There was a slight pause and Brian thought she'd dropped the phone until she roared, "You idiot – I gave you a lift this morning!"

"Err, in that case," said Brian, gobsmacked with embarrassment. "Do you think you could come and pick me up? Darling? Please?"

"Certainly *darling*," replied Brenda, "just as soon as YOU convince the police that I have not stolen your car..."

Hey ho! We're only human and sometimes it's easy to jump to the wrong conclusion. Maybe sometimes we should take life just a little more slowly, stop and think before we act, take a deep breath, count to ten, and remember to send up a quick prayer when things appear to have gone wrong. God always wants to be a part of our life, during the happy moments and the sad moments and yes even during the senior moments.

Father God, sometimes we make the most ridiculous mistakes.
Thank you that you understand us, you know us inside out,
and you still love us.

You know you're getting older if...

You remember when petrol stations actually had attendants who put the petrol in your car, took your money and brought back the change.

●

You remember Green Shield Stamps.

●

You remember waking up to a gurgling Teasmade.

●

You remember having a wireless, not a radio, and certainly none of these iPods or thingamajigs…

●

You remember when putting things online meant hanging out the washing.

●

You remember when there were only two TV channels and they were in black and white.

●

You remember searching for a telephone box to say you'd be late home.

●

You remember the arrival of twin-tub washing machines and thought they were the greatest time-saving invention ever.

You remember taking snapshots
of friends and family
with a Brownie box camera.

●

You remember luncheon vouchers.

●

You remember the joy of setting up
a projector and screen
to watch a cine film of your holiday.

●

You remember a time when pizzas
weren't delivered but milk was.

●

You remember when mobile phones
were the size of a brick.

The right direction?

Thomas said to him, "Lord, we don't know where you are going, so how can we know the way?" Jesus answered, "I am the way and the truth and the life."
John 14:5-6 (NIV)

●

Esme doesn't like visiting places on her own. Not only that, her map-reading skills are non-existent and her technical know-how is even worse, so sat nav is out of the question.

Enter stage left, Moira who, how should I put this, *probably hasn't the best memory in the world*. Little wonder then, that when Esme asked Moira to accompany and direct her to a garden fete some 18 miles distant we were rather concerned. Despite our reservations, Moira was only too happy to oblige. She assured us she knew the place well. The hosts were former neighbours and she had visited them a few times over the years.

That afternoon they set off with a toot of the horn and a wave of the hand; two senior ladies out for a happy excursion into the countryside. What could possibly go wrong? Hmm.

I bumped into Moira the following day. "Did you enjoy the fete?" I asked brightly. "We didn't get there," she said with a sigh. "I couldn't remember the way. Ridiculous. I know exactly where it is, I just couldn't find it."

I sympathised. "So where did you end up?"

"We drove around for hours," Moira replied. "We eventually pitched up in the next county and stopped for a cream tea at a lovely old tea shop. It was rather pleasant, actually!" Then she added, brightening perceptibly, "Probably better than the fete!"

Knowing which path to take is a decision we face many times during our lives. I often think it would be handy to have a split personality; one to take the 'safe' option and one to take the more adventurous route. Would both personalities end up in the same place, I wonder?

I believe that God has a way mapped out for me, though I suspect I miss his signposts frequently. Will I still end up where he wants me? I hope so. I may have a slightly harder time getting there and I might take longer but God won't let the diversions be wasted.

We meet different people at different stages of our journey. They all have something to teach us and our experience is all the richer for it. Human free-will means that sometimes we'll lose our way, but God is there at every turn, watching our progress and, if we ask, he will guide us back onto the 'right road'. What's more, he has a warm welcome awaiting us at journey's end.

AC

As long as I look to you to lead me, you will bring me home.
Thank you, Lord.

In His image

So God created human beings, making them to be like himself.
He created them male and female...
Genesis 1:27 (GNT)

●

When my granddaughter was born she looked so much like her father it was uncanny. She had Gary's eyes, his hair, his smile, even his little toes. (There's a small gap between their little toes and the other four, in case you're wondering...) In fact, it was hard to see how she resembled her mum, something our daughter was a tad disconcerted about!

As I write, little Amber is eight months old. We are gradually beginning to see some characteristics from our side of the family emerging but she is still very much like her daddy.

Of course, as Amber grows and changes, different facets of both parents will start to emerge. She is already the unique creation God intended her to be, but it will be interesting to see whether she will have mum or dad's temperament and whose mannerisms she will exhibit. Hopefully, it will be all the endearing, positive ones from both but I reckon that's asking a bit much.

Part of the excitement of meeting a new baby is trying to discern which parent he or she takes after. We scrutinise the poor infant's face, searching every pore for signs of ma and pa. Without knowing it, we are already 'moulding' the new arrival into someone we want or expect them to be.

The Bible tells us that we are all made in the image of God. Not that we have God's eyebrows or nostrils (or perhaps we have; I can't wait to find out!), but it refers to our innermost spirit, the purest, truest aspect of our being. It is our spirit that, given the chance, responds to *his* voice and connects with *his* spirit. It is who we truly are; the person we were born to be.

The demands of life, along with people's expectations of us, can crush our spirit and we become shadows of our God-intended self. But if we nourish our inner being and give it time and space to listen to the Creator's voice, we will grow in his likeness. So, take a moment to yourself and just 'Be still' – God wants you to know him, draw close to him and become like him. *AC*

Thank you, Father, that you offer new life to everyone.
May we grow closer to you and become more like you.

Age is just a number...
(Well actually it's a word)

Age is a question of mind over matter, if you don't mind it doesn't matter.

•

Maybe we should start referring to ages as levels – it sounds so impressive to say "I have reached level 60 in the game of life."

•

Age is a relative term. All my relatives keep reminding me how old I am.

•

Where does it say we have to act our age?
As long as I'm happy and I'm not hurting anyone, I will act whatever age I like.

•

Age doesn't make you forgetful;
having far too many silly things to remember makes you forgetful.

•

I've reached the age where my train of thought often leaves the station without me.

•

If things get better with age, then I'm approaching magnificent!

•

What's the best thing about reaching the age of 100?
Very little peer pressure.

•

No woman should ever be quite accurate about her age it – looks so calculating.

Oscar Wilde 1854–1900, Irish writer

Of course I don't know how to act my age. I've never been this age before.

The secret to staying young is to live honestly, eat slowly, and lie about your age.

Lucille Ball 1911–1989, American actress and comedienne

●

You're never too old to become younger.

Mae West 1893–1980, American actress and singer

●

I do wish I could tell you my age, but it's impossible, it keeps changing all the time.

Greer Garson 1904–1996, British actress

●

Old age is no place for sissies.

Bette Davis 1908–1989, American actress

Lost and found

I can never forget you! I have written your name on the palms of my hands.
Isaiah 49:16 (GNT)

●

Did you hear the story about Prime Minister, David Cameron, his wife Sam Cam and his daughter Nancy? A few years ago, when the Camerons were the first family, they all went out for a Sunday drink in a local pub near Chequers. Mum and Dad and their three children – Nancy then aged eight, Arthur, six, and 22-month-old Florence.

On leaving the pub, Mr Cameron went home in one car with his bodyguards and thought Nancy was with his wife and their other children in another car. Meanwhile, Mrs Cameron had assumed her elder daughter was with her father and she went home with just the two younger children. The mistake was not discovered until they all got home. What a nightmare!

When Sam Cam returned to collect Nancy a quarter of an hour later, she found her happily helping the staff and not at all worried!

Of course, David Cameron was an extremely busy man, Prime Minister of the country, surrounded by lots of folk asking questions, wanting answers, making demands on his time, so I guess it's not surprising that sometimes he forgot something or someone. And I guess that life as the First Lady of Number 10 was probably pretty hectic too. I gather that Nancy enjoys retelling the story of when her muddle-aged parents totally forgot her – well, wouldn't you?

I'm so glad that God never ever forgets us! He's also surrounded by lots of folk asking questions, wanting answers, making demands on his time – just think how many people send up prayers every day – but happily God is God, omnipotent, all-seeing and all-knowing, whereas the UK Prime Minister is only human. Our Father God has got the whole world in his hands and yet he never ever forgets us. That's a comforting thought.

Father God, you always know where we are and what we're doing,
you never lose us and you never forget us. Thank you for your loving care.

Muddle-age mix-up

Sarah first discovered that she was muddle-aged when she decided to make homemade soup after the roast lunch by simmering the chicken bones to make stock. An hour later she picked up a colander and strained all the liquid through a sieve and straight down the plug hole. Oops! Result: dry bones and no soup!

●

Mary came out of the swimming pool and put her glasses on. The whole world felt blurry and fuzzy, was she wearing someone else's glasses? Was she ill? No… she was just suffering from muddle-age! She had worn contact lenses so she could see in the pool, and then put her glasses on top.

●

The pipe under Jon's kitchen sink was leaking badly so he put a washing up bowl underneath to catch the drips while he rang the plumber. When it was full, he pulled out the bowl and emptied it down the sink! Duh!

●

Busy mum, Sharon, cycled into town to do her shopping, chained up her bike outside the supermarket and filled a bag with groceries. She then set off for home and was halfway there before remembering she'd come by bike.

●

After lots of careful planning and six months of enthusiastic digging, 75 muddle-aged prisoners completely failed to escape from Saltillo Prison in Mexico. They had designed a tunnel that would take them to the other side of the prison wall and freedom. Strangely, their tunnel took an unexpected turning and on 18 April 1976 they came up in the nearby courtroom where many of them had previously been sentenced. The astonished judges quickly returned all 75 convicts to jail!

Steve, a somewhat scatty teacher, went to an office shop to photocopy a bunch of worksheets for his students. He didn't set up the machine correctly and had to wait while dozens of blank sheets came out. He then paid for them all and left the shop quickly as he was too embarrassed to explain that he'd put the original document on the screen upside down.

●

Sally has decided to set the password on her home computer as INCORRECT, so whenever she forgets her password the computer will say…
Your Password is INCORRECT.

●

Actor Manager Herbert Beerbohm Tree once hailed a taxi to take him home from his theatre. He got in the back where he engrossed himself in reading a manuscript. After a few minutes the taxi driver said, "Where to, Guv?" to which he replied…
"Do you really think I'd give my address to the likes of you?"

You remember a time when
you could go to the cinema for the
price of a first class stamp today.

You know you're getting older if...

You remember getting off the sofa and walking across the lounge
to change channels on the television.

•

You recall a time when ordering a coffee was either with or without milk and sugar, not
a question of choosing between cappuccino, espresso, Americano, latte, mocha, etc.

•

You produce a cheque book and pen to pay for your shopping and the checkout
operator doesn't know how to proceed.

•

You select the largest print possible on your e-reader and your kids laugh.

•

Your teenage heartthrob now has grey hair and grandchildren.

•

You look in the mirror and your mother/father stares back at you.

•

You buy shoes based on how they feel, rather than how they look.

•

Those edgy tunes your parents hated are now golden oldies on Radio 2.

The best seat in the house

"What I'm saying is, if you walk around with your nose in the air,
you're going to end up flat on your face.
But if you're content to be simply yourself, you will become more than yourself."
Luke 14:11 (The Message)

●

Whilst not a ditherer, I find I have a growing tendency to change my mind as I get older. Maybe it's just me, but I like to tell myself it's a symptom of muddle-age.

In our house, we can take ages to decide where to go for a day out, only for me to change my mind as soon as we get in the car. By the time we've left the driveway, chances are I'm favouring the original destination once more.

However, its cafes and restaurants that my long-suffering husband dreads the most. We'll choose our spot but, as soon as we're seated, I'll decide, "That table over there is better", and so we decamp. My husband knows that if he goes to the Gents before ordering, there's a good chance he won't be able to find me when he gets back because I'll have moved again.

It's even been known for us to have moved between ordering and the food arriving as I will have seen a table that's cleaner – quieter – better lit – or has a better view.

It's natural to want the best table available when we are paying to dine out. Very few of us would choose the noisiest, dirtiest, most hemmed-in table given the choice. We're (hopefully) a little more tactful when we're invited as someone's guest, though we like to think we'll be offered a good position.

Jesus turned 'Seat Selection' into an illustration of how we should behave in life. He cautioned that if we're conceited and arrogant and grab the best seat in the house for ourselves, then we might just find ourselves embarrassed and humiliated (Luke 14:8–11). On the other hand, if we put others first and look after their comfort and their needs, then we might well be pleasantly surprised when it comes to dining at his heavenly banquet.

So… next time I'm in a restaurant I'll choose a good seat, but I won't tread on any toes or elbow my way to the very best seat. [Phew!] That was my husband breathing a sigh of relief.

Time and again Lord, you turn our selfish values on their head
and honour the humble in heart.
Keep reminding me to put the comfort of others first, I pray.

Just keep smiling...

•

Be cheerful no matter what; pray all the time; thank God no matter what happens.
This is the way God wants you who belong to Christ Jesus to live.
1 Thessalonians 5:16–18 (The Message)

I had spent months tracking down the perfect pair of pink shoes for my niece's wedding! They had style without threatening to cripple me. I'd be able to walk rather than teeter up the church path, and my heels wouldn't sink into the lawn as I posed for family photos.

Just before we left for the 300-mile journey, I put them safely in a carrier bag in the boot of the car. Having searched every shoe shop within a 30-mile radius, I needed to be sure they'd definitely been packed. My husband was loading the cases just as our eldest daughter arrived. She was travelling with us and, as usual, had brought enough cases for a fortnight's holiday instead of the two nights we had planned. My husband hurriedly transferred her bags to the boot of our car and off we went.

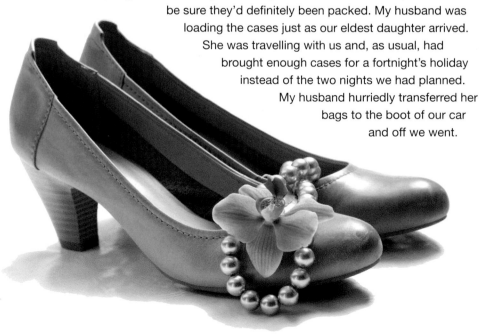

It was only when everything was unpacked in the hotel that I realised my shoes were missing. A thorough search of rooms and car ensued. Nothing. And then the penny dropped; my husband had repacked the car in order to fit in our daughter's luggage. As far as he was concerned, everything he had packed was accounted for.

All I had was my well-worn trainers so, at ten o'clock that night, my daughter and I drove to the nearest supermarket to buy substitute shoes. I found a pair of cheap flat white sandals and wore them the next day.

I had been sorely tempted to make a huge fuss – to blame my husband, my daughter, even the dog, for my shoes being left behind – but, at the end of the day, would I let their absence spoil our enjoyment of a family wedding? No! And, as soon as I made a conscious decision to grin and bear it, I felt my downcast sole heeled.

God wants us to 'give thanks in all circumstances' so here goes… I'm thankful that I didn't have to wear my trainers, I'm thankful that a late night supermarket was open and, if I'm honest, I'm thankful that my cheap sandals were more comfortable than my posh pink shoes!

AC

Lord, help me to cultivate an attitude of gratitude,
to look on the bright side of life
and to treat difficulties as a challenge rather than a disaster.

•

PS: I will never be over the hill –
I don't have the right shoes, and I'm too tired to climb it.

Father God,

As we grow older, year by year,
May we see you more clearly,
May we love you more dearly, and
May we follow you more nearly.
Year by year, help us to grow closer to you.

Amen

Adapted from the prayer of St Richard, Bishop of Chichester,
written in the 13th century